Streets of Cardiff

Roger Davies

Ian Allan PUBLISHING

Introduction

I want you to remember one word: Nantgarw. This is a small town, now home to the National Museum of Wales transport collection but once host to a coal mine. The nearest one to Cardiff. It's 10 miles away; there are no coal mines in Cardiff, and never have been.

Coal was a bit important, though. Let's go back. The River Taff breaks its way out of the South Wales mountains through a spectacular gorge near Taff's Well. About 2,000 years ago, on some swampy land where the river met the sea, a hamlet grew up, and not a lot happened for a very long time. In the second half of the 18th century coal and ironstone were discovered in them thar hills, and a thriving business exporting the stuff grew up. There was only one way out — via the Taff Gorge — and when you reached the sea, there was Cardiff. It was the obvious place to export coal and ironstone from and also to build steel works, to use some of it up. Mule carts started the trade, the Glamorganshire Canal opening in 1794 and the Taff Vale Railway in 1840. Cardiff's first dock, the Bute West, opened in 1839. These latter two would have been celebrated by Cardiff's 1836 population of 8,000. Their existence — and the impact of subsequent developments — meant that by 1888 the population had risen to no less than 123,000.

In essence Cardiff was a transport town. All types of transport were to be found, and it must have been a bustling and exciting time. This growing population soon required transport of its own, and horse-bus services appeared in 1845, to be followed by horse trams in 1872.

In the days of horse propulsion one of the pioneers was a certain Solomon Andrews, an entrepreneur on a truly staggering scale. He had interests not only in tramways but also in bakery, medicine, undertaking, shops, furniture, department stores, skating rinks, cinemas, cars and car hire and collieries. Some of his interests stretched as far as Australia. He also built horse buses, and his Patent Omnibus of 1882 is regarded as a classic.

By the end of the 19th century the new Cardiff County Borough Council felt that the expanding public-transport services were not being run in the best interests of ratepayers. In 1898 it obtained Parliamentary powers to take over all the tramways in its area and wanted to forge ahead with the then revolutionary new electric trams. In 1900 a new General Manager, Arthur Ellis, was appointed, and he put together a grand scheme to introduce these wonders to the town. On 1 January 1902 the Borough Council took over most of the tramways (the remaining route joining them in 1903). By 1 May 1902 Arthur Ellis was able to launch the first 12 electric trams, and by 1904 the last horse trams had gone, horse buses lingering until 1909. By the time Cardiff became a city, in 1905, 131 electric trams were providing services focused mainly on linking all areas to the busy docks.

Having warmly embraced electric trams, the City Council was less enthusiastic about motor buses, refusing them entry in 1907. But it couldn't hold out against progress forever, and the new-fangled things were let in from 1910. Following the upsurge in such vehicles after World War 1 the Council started operating its own from 1920.

To take account of the numerous bridges that plagued the city (owing to the

---

Front cover: A classic scene, viewed from the Castle, which neatly encapsulates *Streets of Cardiff*. Recorded in 1963, it features a two-way Queen Street (it's now pedestrianised!) and a fantastic collection of vehicles and fashions. Two trolleybuses — one newly painted, the other ...... er, not — flank one of the 20 AEC Regent III double-decks of 1950, which, well into their twilight years, worked (as here) the lengthy route 50 right across the city. A Western Welsh dual-purpose vehicle, believed to be one of four Park Royal-bodied AEC Reliances acquired in 1956 from Green's of Haverfordwest, sneaks past on the left, heading for Kingsway. *Robert Alderson Smith*

Previous page: Cardiff's splendid City Hall, opened in 1902, is a fitting symbol of the city. When Queen Street became one-way, in 1965, eastbound traffic, including trolleybuses, was re-routed in front of it. No 274 passes in April 1968, in a scene so quiet as to be unimaginable today! If you were looking for a home for the Welsh Assembly, where better than this? *Alan Jarvis*

First published 2006

ISBN (10) 0 7110 3098 7
ISBN (13) 978 0 7110 3098 5

© Ian Allan Publishing Ltd 2006

Published by Ian Allan Publishing

an imprint of Ian Allan Publishing Ltd, Hersham, Surrey KT12 4RG

Printed in England by Ian Allan Printing Ltd, Hersham, Surrey KT12 4RG

Code: 0601/B

Visit the Ian Allan Publishing website at www.ianallanpublishing.com

multiplicity of railway lines), a unique design of low-height covered-top tramcar was introduced, this being named after the General Manager, Mr R. L. Horsfield. Ultimately 81 such trams entered service, giving Cardiff a very modern fleet, but by 1939 the system was becoming worn out. The dynamic General Manager who had joined in 1928, one William Forbes, had demonstrated the flexibility and financial success of diesel-engined motor buses during the 1930s, and in January 1939 it was decided to do away with the trams as quickly as possible. There was, however, to be one twist to the story, for in May of that year political influences deemed that replacement should not be with motor buses but with electric trolleybuses, thus ensuring the continued use of locally produced fuel.

Whatever he may have felt, Mr Forbes set to with a will, drawing up grand plans for trolleybuses, and had these been fulfilled the system would have been second in size only to London's. However, World War 2 intervened, the trolleybuses did not start until 1 March 1942, and postwar shortages meant the trams struggled on until February 1950, by which time they were extremely decrepit.

A splendid trolleybus system, using unique vehicles designed for a 'pay as you enter' flat-fare system (albeit used as such for only three years) was built up, and the trolleys themselves lasted until 1970. The last major extension, and one that took trolleybuses much further than the trams had ever gone, into Ely, opened in 1955, the year Cardiff became the capital city of Wales. Despite its relatively brief existence Cardiff's trolleybus system is remembered with great fondness; there are many of us who recall the twin staircases of most of the buses, which allowed you to run downstairs at the front when the conductor came upstairs at the back!

Since 1970 Cardiff has been served only by motor buses, but over the years a huge variety has been used. From 1972, the long-established (and much-missed) livery of crimson lake and cream was replaced by orange, and in 1980 the last conductors made their final journeys on route 16 to Snowden Road, in Ely. In 1999 Cardiff Bus, the 'arm's length' company set up under the terms of the 1985 Transport Act, adopted the city's

corporate colours of Burges blue and cream.

But Cardiff wasn't just about Cardiff Corporation buses. The city was served by a variety of other municipally owned undertakings, including Newport, West Mon (based in Blackwood), Caerphilly and Merthyr Tydfil, along with area operators such as Western Welsh, Red & White, Rhondda and the impressive Neath & Cardiff Luxury Coaches. Other companies and numerous private firms visited for major attractions, such as rugby matches at the Arms Park and exhibitions at Sophia Gardens. For the bus enthusiast, Cardiff in the '60s couldn't be beaten, and I remember my shock at travelling elsewhere and finding cities served by just a handful of companies.

This book does not seek to be a definitive guide to buses that could be seen in Cardiff, but many of the images have never been published before. Inevitably, the Central Bus Station, opened in 1954, was the setting for many a bus photograph, and it is impossible not to include a number at this location.

Customhouse Street has changed out of all recognition, as this early-1960s photograph reveals. There is a fantastic variety of vehicles, the Fordson truck on the left and the typical British Road Services eight-wheel Leyland on the right being just two examples. In the distance are a Red & White Albion single-deck and a Cardiff Regent V; we can only wonder at how they fought their way through. At this time the street was the centre of the wholesale fruit-and-vegetable market. *John Woodward*

Below: The first of three tinted postcards giving a feel of Edwardian Cardiff and depicting examples of the first trams. No 67 stands at the top of St Mary Street, when roads were shared with people! *R. W. A. Jones collection, courtesy Keith Walker*

Right: Queen Street, with pedestrians spilling over into the road. Ultimately they won, as the street is now pedestrianised. Look at the wonderful signs and the ornate overhead wire supports in the middle of the road. *R. W. A. Jones collection, courtesy Keith Walker*

Below right: A flavour of Suburban Cardiff in the early 20th century, with a tram making its way along Newport Road. *R. W. A. Jones collection, courtesy Keith Walker*

Also the clear bias towards trolleybuses means that the book should perhaps be called *Trolleybus Streets of Cardiff*! I make no apology.

But you forget that places have a certain individual character about them, and Cardiff does, by the bucketload. From the imposing Civic Centre (surely the rightful home of the Welsh Assembly — not some gin palace 'down the docks') to the genteel avenues, terraces of villas and parklands, it has a feel all of its own. It is very difficult to capture that character, but I have tried to do so using the wide variety of pictures sent to me. These are in some sort of order, feature loads of trolleybuses and bring back fond memories for me. I hope they do the same for those of you who know Cardiff …… and, for those of you who don't, I hope you enjoy the ride!

Acknowledgements
The selection of photos is designed to give a flavour of Cardiff in days that are not too far away but actually farther than you think. There's no definitive aim with the book, so some of you will groan: "Oh no! Why isn't *that* in?". But I hope you will also — as I have done — gain great pleasure from memories rekindled by these scenes and the vehicles in them.

My thanks go to all those who sent me material. In the end I've plumped for what I believe to be largely unseen work, so particular thanks to Alan Jarvis, Andy Smith Photography, Mike Street, Keith Walker, Andrew Wiltshire and John Woodward. Cardiff's transport heritage is kept alive by the Cardiff & South Wales Trolleybus Project, at 211 Hillrise, Llanedeyrn, Cardiff CF32 6UQ, and the Cardiff Transport Preservation Group, on www.ctpg.co.uk. Please support them if you can.

Finally, any opinions, indulgences and mistakes are mine.

Roger Davies
Linton, Kent
September 2005

Right: So how do we get there? Easy — it's just down the M4. Well, not always; before that bit of the M4 that went over the first Severn crossing opened in September 1966, the lowest crossing-point was Gloucester. Without any motorways or dual-carriageways as we know them today, Cardiff could be mildly referred to as 'a bit cut off'. You *could* get across; these tiny ferries shuttled to and fro roughly where the first Severn Bridge is now, but, as *Severn Princess* — here unloading on the Welsh side — shows, they didn't carry many vehicles, and queues of several hours were commonplace. There was another way, the one we used on our marathon trips for South Coast holidays, and that was the train: you put your car onto an open wagon and settled down in a carriage at Severn Tunnel Junction, and the train would chuff through the Severn Tunnel and deposit you at Pilning — all very exciting, and exactly what Channel Tunnel freight shuttles do today! *Robert Alderson Smith*

SEVERN PRINCESS   SEVERN PRINCESS

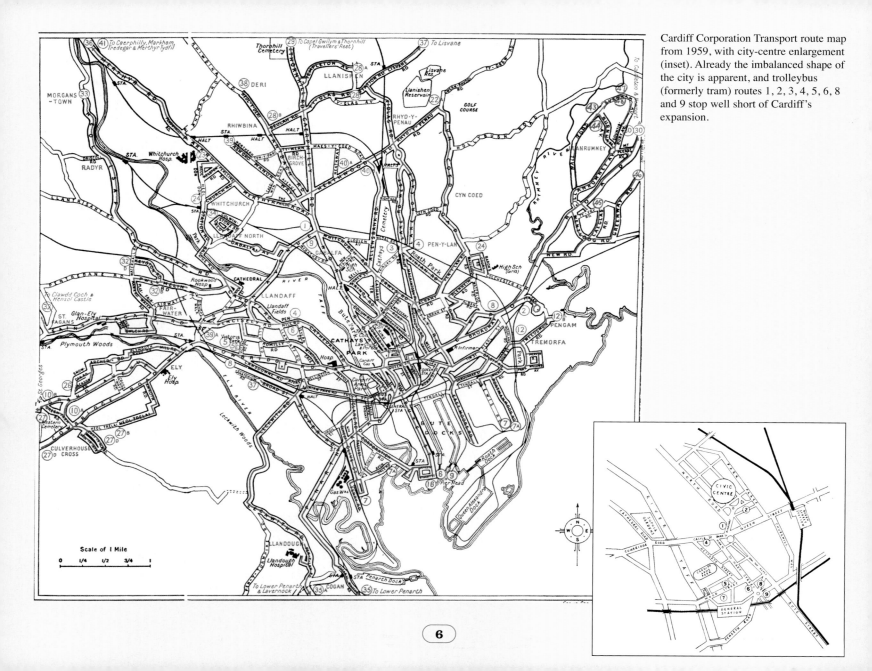

Cardiff Corporation Transport route map from 1959, with city-centre enlargement (inset). Already the imbalanced shape of the city is apparent, and trolleybus (formerly tram) routes 1, 2, 3, 4, 5, 6, 8 and 9 stop well short of Cardiff's expansion.

At the Centre

A brief trip around Cardiff's city centre

How better to start than with No 1? Cardiff Corporation 1, a 1950 AEC Regent III with locally built Bruce bodywork, lurks near the entrance to the central bus station in 1965. Behind it a Western Welsh Leyland Atlantean barrels into the bus station, pursued by a Red & White Bristol MW coach. In the background a Cardiff trolleybus bound for Pier Head is about to pass the Corporation Transport's head office before crossing the bridge over the River Taff whose weakness would, in but a few months, bring about their demise on these routes. Also visible are the Empire Swimming Pool, built in 1958 for that year's Empire Games, and the telephone exchange, both now swept away to make room for the Millennium Stadium. The offices of long-gone BEA and Cambrian Airways and still-current Aer Lingus were located within the bus-station buildings, themselves now threatened with demolition. *John Woodward*

Above: Rainy day in Wood Street! The bus station was not big enough to accommodate all the buses terminating in the city centre, so there were a number of other termini. For example, no trolleybus services used the bus station, but they did call outside, as demonstrated by BUT 228 on a Sunday-morning 5A to Victoria Park in 1965. The trolleybus on the left, BUT 271, is heading for Llandaff Fields on service 6; beyond it is the Tabernacle, and to the left of that is Havelock Street, terminus for the 10A/B trolleybuses to/from Ely. *John Woodward*

Right: Around the corner, at the eastern end of Wood Street, was St Mary Street where BUT trolleybus 274 is seen waiting to depart for Roath Park in April 1968, shortly before succumbing to motor buses similar to the Alexander-bodied Guy Arab approaching. Many of the buildings are still familiar today, albeit now used for different purposes. A. J. Anstee, the florist, was a Cardiff institution. *Alan Jarvis*

Above: A little further on is Mill Lane, still with us but much changed! The Cardiff Corporation staff club was located in one of the tall buildings in the background; they may well have got their eggs from the Wenvoe supply! The Corporation was a bit undecided about this location, referring to it as 'Mill Lane' or — as here on AEC Regent V No 387, working route 39 — 'St Mary Street'; the single-deck trolleybuses working the frequent shuttle to the Docks always referred to it as 'Monument'. This shot dates from January 1964, shortly before the single-deck trolleybuses — the last to run in England & Wales — were replaced by motor buses. *Alan Jarvis*

Right: Many routes from the north of the city terminated at Greyfriars Road, on the opposite side of the city centre from the bus station. The name came from an old friary, which was replaced by Cardiff's first (and only very) tall building. Seen here when brand-new in December 1971, 555 was one of 35 Daimler Fleetlines that were the last buses delivered in crimson lake and cream. They were very fast. Drivers loved them. *Mike Street*

Left: A quiet oasis in the bustling city centre was the Windsor Place terminus of service 5 and short workings of various other routes. All were summarily withdrawn in 1965 without replacement, despite being very frequent. Mind you, timetables had not changed since the early '50s, but patronage certainly had, and the very tight left turns into and out of this street were being made more difficult, as here, by parked cars. Thankfully BUT 262, bodied in Cardiff at Pengam Moors by Bruce Coachworks and pictured in 1965, has been preserved and will hopefully appear soon in full working order. The site is now occupied by large office blocks. Actually, it was Windsor Lane … *John Woodward*

Below left: Inside, most Cardiff trolleybuses had this unique two-door, two-staircase arrangement, designed for pay-as-you-enter operation. This latter was pretty revolutionary and was introduced with the first trolleys on 1 March 1942 along with a 1d flat fare, making Cardiff the only place to reduce its fares during the War. The system was abandoned in 1950, and gradually those buses with doors at the front had these panelled over, giving a large standing area. This lovely view of the inside of BUT 262 shows this feature and the front staircase; also the long rear-facing seat, upon which folk would sit gazing at their feet to avoid eye contact with other passengers! Also visible is the neat Cardiff Corporation garter around the fleet number on the front bulkhead. *John Woodward*

Right: But the bus station was the main point, so let's spend some time there to enjoy the variety. 'Meet you at the N&C' was a common cry in Cardiff and referred to this prime site right at the front of the bus station. Here could be found the stunning vehicles of Neath & Cardiff Luxury Coaches — or 'Brown Bombers', as they were known — waiting to whisk you off with great *élan* to Swansea. None of this washed with the National Bus Company, which decreed that the company should be broken up and absorbed into South Wales Transport and Western Welsh; the service thereby lost its identity and very shortly became just any old bus route (vandalism!), and thus another local institution perished for no good reason. Anyway, in a transient stage, having had its N&C monograms crudely stripped away and naff, bland South Wales names applied, is a splendid Harrington-bodied AEC Reliance, one of the first 36-footers, 'at the N&C' in October 1971. *Mike Street*

Left: South Wales was renowned for the number of local authorities which ran their own buses, at its peak totalling nine (two of which were actually two authorities working jointly). Many of these served Cardiff. One that seemed to have great dignity was Merthyr Tydfil. Its splendid No 146, a Leyland PD3, was the last double-deck it bought, joining the fleet in 1966. It doesn't get much better than this, and East Lancs, which built the bodywork, still remains today as one of the very few British bus builders — unlike Merthyr Tydfil Transport, which is long gone. Here in 1971 it's working the joint service between the two centres, which ran every 20 minutes and was worked jointly by Cardiff and Merthyr, which called it the 20, and Rhondda Transport, which called it the 100. Don't ask me! *Mike Street*

Above: Newport was another of the local authorities and also another to move from double-deckers to single-deckers in the early '70s. In a blast from the past it moved onto a flat-fare system, but the fare was more than a penny! It also caused a stir by having a large fleet of unusual Metro-Scania buses, of which No 58 is seen working on the joint service with Cardiff to Newport. This local-authority fleet remains to this day and is still painted green, albeit a more sombre shade than this. *Mike Street*

Left: Cardiff was also home to the Western Welsh company, a huge outfit stretching right across South Wales. The name was not geographical — indeed, it would have been misleading — but was derived from the Great Western Railway, which had a hand in setting it up. With over 700 buses and a cast of thousands across its area, it was a major part of the Cardiff scene but has vanished virtually without trace. It was well known for building up probably the largest fleet of Leyland's lightweight Tiger Cub, finally totalling some 347. This late Park Royal-bodied bus is seen in 1972 in the smart red livery with rather agreeable fleetname of the time. The orange diamond below the trafficator denotes that it was allocated to the Penarth Road depot in Cardiff. *Mike Street*

Right: The Penarth Road depot of Western Welsh, the orange-diamond one, was conveniently located only a few minutes from the bus station. It's still there, but it hasn't seen a bus in ages. For some reason in 1965 Western Welsh decided to paint its coaches and dual-purpose vehicles blue and cream — very nice, but one must ask why. Showing off this livery at said depot in September 1972 is a dual-purpose Leyland Leopard/Willowbrook, one of the first short Leopards bought by Western Welsh, the company having finally forsaken the Tiger Cub. Shortly afterwards this delightful livery was replaced by drab NBC red. Didn't see the point then, still don't. *John Wiltshire*

Right: Commonly managed Rhondda Transport of Porth followed Western Welsh's lead and painted its coaches and dual-purpose vehicles green and cream. Even nicer, but, well, you still ask why. These were much rarer, as Rhondda had only a handful. By 1972, when this photograph was taken, Rhondda had been fully absorbed into the Western Welsh fleet, long Leopard/Willowbrook 320 becoming 2320. *Mike Street*

Another major company to work into Cardiff was Red & White, based in Chepstow but with a depot in Cardiff at Gelligaer Street, behind Maindy sports stadium; on school sports day it provided a useful early escape route. As part of the State-owned Tilling group, its buses were pretty standardised, but these 21 Bristol RESL buses dating from 1967 were relatively unusual. This style of rounded-front body was quite nice too. RS1267 in R&W's batty fleet-numbering system told the engineers it was short and had a rear engine (you'd think they'd have noticed) and that it was the 12th bus delivered in 1967. As if you'd want to know. By the time of this 1972 shot it had gained NBC livery and really *was* red and white! *Mike Street*

South Wales was famous for the number of small private companies running bus services. Cardiff was rather exempt from this general rule, but Thomas of Barry provided one bus on the route linking the two, which was operated jointly with Western Welsh. The route ran via Dinas Powis, where a low bridge precluded the use of double-decks. Seen in April 1971, Thomas's Leyland Leopard/Willowbrook ATG 708J was very similar to WW buses on the service. WW crews always referred to the 304 route as the 'low road', the 'top road' being that via Wenvoe.
John Wiltshire

Left: Away from the bus station, let's have a wander around the city centre. At the castle end of St Mary Street it decides to become High Street and turns onto another street that changes name for no particular reason, from Castle Street to Duke Street. Anyway, here in 1973 dual-door Daimler Fleetline 544 swings into the fourth from the second. Don't worry, I'll not be asking questions. *Mike Street*

Above: And entering Duke Street after making that turn we get a nice view along it, with the castle on our left and Queen Street straight ahead. The bus in this 1963 view is a 1953 D. J. Davies-bodied Guy, one of 15. There are some splendid lorries and cars to enjoy and a police 'phone box of the type that would really have challenged Dr Who. *Robert Alderson Smith*

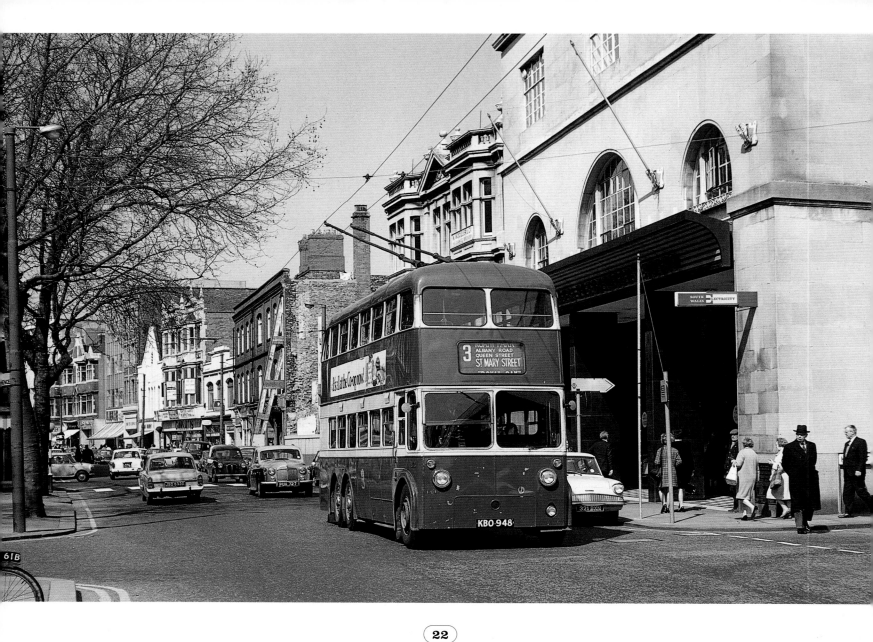

Left: At the end of Queen Street was a crossroads, and the turn to the south led you ultimately to Mill Lane (or Monument, if you prefer). Trolleybuses terminating in St Mary Street used this one-way loop to turn around, and BUT/East Lancs 275, one of the final, 1955 batch of trolleybuses, passes through delightful Hayes, with its tea stand and Central Library, in 1968. This area is now tastefully pedestrianised. *Alan Jarvis*

Above: And now back to the end of Queen Street, which by the time of this July 1967 view was a one-way street. BUT trolleybus 255, with rather tastelessly modified front windows, is followed by an unmodified example as it passes a Guy Arab V motor bus working a cross-city journey on route 8 from the Royal Oak to Victoria Park. The sports car seems to be winning. *Alan Jarvis*

In 1965 specially polished trolleybus 275 takes an official party of Cardiff councillors and transport hierarchy on an inspection trip along the newly erected wiring up Kingsway to pass in front of the City Hall through the newly constructed link road (now known as Stuttgarterstraße) and down Dumfries Place. This all came about as a result of Queen Street's becoming one-way westbound (see previous picture) but had the advantage of bringing trolleybuses in sight of the Civic Centre (see page 1). The overhead-wire supports were painted a light-stone colour (rather than the usual green), as this was thought — quite rightly — to be more in keeping with the area. In the background, just in case of problems, is Bedford tower wagon 911 BUH. There's a great selection of cars — notice the Triumph Herald (the Dinky Toys version of which, in blue and green, was released on my birthday; I passed my driving test in a real one) — and on-street parking right in the city centre! Also in view are the back of a D. J. Davies-bodied Guy bus, very much at home on the 40A/B route, and a Daimler CVG6 on a 39, matching its typical Cardiff beer advert with the pub it is passing. *John Woodward*

A few minutes later 275 causes a stir as it becomes the first trolleybus to pass the imposing City Hall under electric power. *John Woodward*

One of the more curious results of the new one-way system was a lay-by outside the City Hall for coaches to drop off passengers. This had the effect of them being marooned on a little island next to the carriageway and was not hugely popular. In this November 1973 view it is being used to park coaches bringing folk to a Rugby International. This one is a rare Weymann-bodied AEC Reliance owned by D Coaches of Swansea. It was new to Western Welsh in 1961 and has the styling of those days. Crews called them 'Sabrinas' … *Mike Street*

Right: Cardiff Castle forms a splendid backdrop to many Cardiff pictures, but these are generally taken from the front. It is easy to miss just how impressive it looks from the side, and this picture on a wet March day in 1974 does it justice. Kingsway at this point is much changed today, but the Castle is just as grand. The two Fleetlines in overall adverts are both promoting Barclaycard, MCW-bodied 476 (left) in an earlier version, Willowbrook 549 (right) in a later scheme; the third bus, an Alexander-bodied Guy Arab V, is just in the ' 'orrible orange' fleet colours of the day. *Mike Street*

Below right: In the late 1950s a revolution in double-deck bus design took place in that the engine was moved to the rear. This allowed greater seating capacity and a flat floor, and the driver could supervise people getting on and off. Cardiff was a bit slow off the mark with this type of bus but in April 1966 decided to order 32 of them, at a total cost of £256,767 — about the price of two new double-deckers in 2005! The first 16, Cardiff's first rear-engined buses, entered service in 1967 and had MCW bodywork of a style favoured by Manchester. No 481 gives us another angle on the Castle as it makes its way along Kingsway in April 1974. *Mike Street*

Left: A classic view of Cardiff Castle's ornate clock tower, with probably the most picturesque bus-stop locations in the city. What is unusual is the bus, as these stops were the preserve of Corporation buses. Very much an interloper, therefore, is Rhondda Transport 440, a forward-entrance MCW-bodied AEC Regent V typical of that fleet. Seen in June 1965, with period adverts to match, it was working a private hire. *John Wiltshire*

Down the Docks

Once the powerhouse of Cardiff, now changed beyond recognition

Cardiff was a bustling port built on the coal trade. When that declined, other cargoes had to be found, and this 1968 view shows MG sports cars and ex-London Transport buses being exported to the USA. One time RLH 4 and 6 were on their way to join Ye Olde Kansas City Touring Association; both had always been green in their London days! And just look at how casual the whole thing is, with a family getting a close-up view. Happy days! *Robert Alderson Smith*

Left: Perhaps the most famous of Cardiff's trolleybuses were the six single-deckers used on the Monument–Pier Head route. This passed along Bute Street through an area known as Tiger Bay, immortalised in film and by Shirley Bassey. Even though Cardiff's double-deck trolleybuses were built to a low height, they still could not get under Bute Street railway bridge, hence the need for single-decks. Here, in December 1963, BUT/East Lancs 241 reverses at Pier Head, where Company instructions stated that the conductor should stand in the roadway to give signals to the driver, using a whistle! *John Wiltshire*

Below left: Pulling onto the terminal stop at Pier Head (a scene much changed today), 241 clearly shows the door arrangement. The first five single-deckers were also originally fitted with doors at the front, for pay-as-you-enter working. This route was originally run by noisy old second-hand trolleybuses, bought from Pontypridd and christened 'doodlebugs'. Unfairly, this nickname stuck with these much more sophisticated buses. By 1963, when this photograph was taken, they were about to be replaced with much bigger double-deck motor buses that could get under the bridge. *John Wiltshire*

Apart from the delight of travelling on a single-deck trolleybus, another very good reason to go to the Pier Head was to board one of P. & A. Campbell's White Funnel paddle-steamers. These whisked you off to the delights of Ilfracombe, Weston-super-Mare and Lundy Island. Here, in 1965, the *Bristol Queen* — the second-largest paddle-steamer in the country — passes Penarth, with Weston in the distance and a boy gone fishing wearing a tie. OK, so not exactly a street of Cardiff, but very much part of the scene! *Robert Alderson Smith*

The single-deck trolleybuses were replaced by big, 70-seater motor buses, and the route linked with service 2 to Pengam, the first trolleybus route to go over to motor buses, in 1962. The terminal loop for the remaining double-deck trolleybus routes to the Pier Head via Grangetown was reversed, which work is seen in progress in 1964 as one of the new Guy buses, 423, showing off its elaborate arrow trafficators, passes tower wagon 911 BUH. The lady carrying the shopping bag would know she was rounding 'Windy Corner' ... indeed, it still is! *John Woodward*

On 16 December 1965 Wood Street bridge, spanning the River Taff near the bus station, was declared weak, and trolleybuses, weighing in at 15½ tons, were immediately banned. The two routes in question, 6 and 9, were split at the city centre, lighter motor buses taking over the southern bit until enough new buses had been delivered to reintroduce the through service, in April 1966. Thus in under two years the Pier Head, which had been served almost exclusively by electric vehicles, lost them all. In this picture (complete with matching car!) BUT trolleybus 222, at the Pier Head on a farewell tour of the Grangetown routes, is being overtaken by the numerically satisfying Guy motor bus 444. These motor buses had bodywork by Alexander of Falkirk — a radical departure for Cardiff and thought to be unique to the city. This section of road has now been swallowed up by Mermaid Quay and the Cardiff Waterfront development, all part of Cardiff Bay. *John Woodward*

Left: Bridges were all part of life for Cardiff's buses, and one of the most impressive was Clarence Road Bridge, linking Grangetown with the docks across the River Taff. Trolleybuses had to observe a 5mph speed limit whilst making their way across, as in this excellent shot of the bridge taken from downriver in May 1965. Built in 1890, the bridge was demolished a century later. *Andrew Wiltshire collection*

Below left: Another view of Clarence Road Bridge, this time featuring Alexander-bodied Guy Arab V bus 448 in June 1970. Note the sign restricting use to one bus at a time. The hole in the bulkhead on the platform of the bus was an additional feature introduced on these buses to hold pushchairs and added £10 10s 0d (£10.50) to the cost of each one! *Andrew Wiltshire collection*

Right: In 1972 three different liveries were tried before orange was settled upon. One was this disturbing turquoise, Fleetline/Willowbrook 550 being the second bus so treated. This view shows its dual-door layout, fashionable when it was new in 1969 but not repeated on subsequent Cardiff double-deckers. When new 550 was also noteworthy in being painted in an overall advert livery — the second in the UK but the first bi-lingual one! Here in July 1972 it's travelling up from the docks to the city along Bute Street, the railway line in the background being about the only recognisable feature today. *John Wiltshire*

Fire!

Lovely, but you didn't want them calling at your house

Left: Cardiff Fire Brigade had some splendid AEC fire engines, one of which is seen in 1965 putting out a fire in Rover Way — an altogether much more rural spot than it is now! By its registration, LTX 855 has come from the Glamorganshire fleet. *John Woodward*

Right: Another of the fabulous AEC fire engines — a Cardiff original — crosses Cardiff Bridge in July 1967. *Alan Jarvis*

Right: The Central Fire Station in Westgate Street was a magnificent structure. Here an immaculate AEC/Merryweather fire engine, complete with City coat of arms, is reversed back in by a very smart crew. *John Wiltshire*

Out and About

A roughly east–west journey across the city

Left: The first trolleybus route to be withdrawn, in 1962, was that to Pengam — the only one to pass the trolleybus depot at Roath. Ironically it came about in order to build a road, Rover Way, to a car-parts factory! Here in January 1963, three trolleybuses gather at the terminus, that nearest the camera being BUT/East Lancs 250. *Alan Jarvis*

Right: Cardiff's first trolleybus on the first route to be abandoned. No 201, a 1942 AEC with Northern Counties bodywork, crosses over the ex-GWR main line on its way to Pengam in April 1962, with views that are much changed today. The 10 buses of this batch had only one door from new; when the City Council enquired whether they could be modified to Cardiff's preferred dual-door layout it was found that the seating capacity would be reduced too much, so they were left alone. *John Wiltshire*

Right: The nearest trolleybuses came to the depot after the Pengam closure was the Royal Oak, about 300 yards away, beyond the railway bridge. BUT 251 turns here in winter sunshine in 1961. The terminus was named after the local pub, still alive and well and famous for its boxing connections. *John Woodward*

Left: Further in towards the city was the busy Newport Road/City Road junction. This unusual view from the roof of Telephone House shows the roofs of two BUT trolleybuses, the nearer one, 216, being the Cardiff standard from the 1948-50 period and the farther one, 275, a 1955 model. Both show the walkway on the roof to attend the booms, and 216 shows the split rear window upstairs, which was used by staff when open to stand on to replace the carbon inserts in the trolleyheads. Guy Arab V motor bus 446 (left) clearly shows the translucent panel down the middle of the roof to bring extra light. *Alan Jarvis*

Above: In April 1968 BUT trolleybus 251 makes its way along City Road in the company of a fine selection of cars (albeit in much less profusion than would be the case today) — fitting really, for it seemed as if every property along this section of road sold second-hand cars! *Alan Jarvis*

Above: After leaving the Roath Park terminus trolleybuses on the 3 and 4 routes ran along Ninian Road, with the expanse of the extensive playing fields to their left. At the junction with Pen-y-lan Road they turned right into Wellfield Road, and BUT 274 — apparently Cardiff's most photographed trolleybus — does just this in 1968. There's also a nice Riley Elf, being pursued by a man in a Trilby! *John Wiltshire*

Right: Coming from Roath Park in July 1967, BUT trolleybus 254 turns from Wellfield Road into Albany Road on its way to the city centre. Pilgrimages to Wellfield Road were commonplace, for here was to be found the fabulous Thayer's ice-cream shop. *Alan Jarvis*

Above: We return now to the Gabalfa route, on which a very smart BUT 213 is seen being pursued by a spectacular ERF truck past Cathays Library in June 1966. Above the entrance (right) is the inscription 'CARNEGIE LIBRARY — FREE TO THE PUBLIC', while the public conveniences (left, complete with Doric columns!) are dated 1934. This fine emporium surely inspired generations to look at books, and the adjoining cemetery ensured that there were no noisy neighbours. *Alan Jarvis*

Right: Looking slightly more careworn, No 213 leaves Gabalfa terminus to head back to the city centre. The terminus was originally across North Road (the main road in the background) but was moved to make way for the construction of the A470 flyover. The Public Works & Town Planning Department paid £2,000 to alter the overhead and £6,000 to demolish two houses in St Mark's Avenue (on the right) to make way for the buses. Can you imagine that today? The work was carried out in 1961, but in the event the flyover wasn't started until several years later. *Alan Jarvis*

In a scene which shows off well suburban villas of the 1920s along with a typical corner shop, Fleetline/Willowbrook 539 approaches the junction of Mackintosh Place and Pen-y-Wain Road on its way to Llanishen via Roath Park in June 1973. *Mike Street*

Above: Right in the north of the city, routes 21 and 23 still link Whitchurch and Rhiwbina and somehow get across the raging torrent that is the A470 just after its junction with the M4. At this point in April 1972 bus 416 makes stately progress across Manor Way in a scene of almost rural calm hardly recognisable today. The bus was one of 12 AEC Regent Vs with East Lancs bodies (this one built at its subsidiary Neepsend in Sheffield) that turned out to be the last AEC double-decks bought, thereby bringing to an end a tradition that stretched back to the '30s. *John Wiltshire*

Left: Pictured in July 1973, Heol Llanishen Fach in Rhiwbina shows us a good example of 1950s and '60s residential architecture. Fleetline 556 also shows British bus-building at its best but rather debased by a garish overall advert livery that really didn't do anything to encourage public-transport usage. Maybe it encouraged insurance … *John Wiltshire*

Above: Being built on the coast, Cardiff could expand in only three directions, and this results in a number of housing estates' being a considerable distance from the city centre. This was how the city outgrew its fixed tram and trolleybus systems and, in all honesty, was an ideal place for motor buses — a fact noted by the Corporation's dynamic General Manager, William Forbes, in the 1930s. He was over-ruled by political considerations which demanded the continued use of home-produced fuel, leading to the introduction of the trolleybuses — which, heart over head, wasn't a bad outcome. Anyway, typical of these estates is Pentrebane, where 526, the first of the dual-door Willowbrook-bodied Fleetlines, is seen at the terminus of the 32D from the city centre via Llandaff in April 1973. The bus had just been painted to celebrate Cardiff's twinning with the French city of Nantes. *Mike Street*

One of the most attractive parts of the trolleybus system was stately Cathedral Road (yes — if you kept going you would ultimately get to the Cathedral in Llandaff, but it was a bit of a step), culminating at the Llandaff Fields terminus. This delightful 1963 picture shows BUT 261, with Cardiff-built Bruce body, making its way up Cathedral Road when this was still mainly residential rather than the posh office area it has since become. No 261 had the dubious honour of being the first of the Cardiff 'Standards' to be withdrawn, but happily the bus behind, Alexander-bodied Crossley 46, is preserved. *Robert Alderson Smith*

Right: BUT trolleybus 271 at the attractive Llandaff Fields terminus, where a special turning-circle was constructed for buses. This one is on the 6, Cardiff's first trolleybus route, which started on 1 March 1942, running from the city to Clarence Road, being extended here on 8 November. Seen in 1966, No 271 is carrying a Kardov Flour advert, which was the first to break the adverts-in-fleet-livery-only rule. School rugby was played at Llandaff Fields, and these buses offered the author — not of a sporting bent — a welcome release after the horrors of the pitch. *John Woodward*

Below: Another view of the Llandaff Fields terminus, this time in June 1965, when road resurfacing had exposed the old tramtracks. The studios of Cardiff's first ITV station, TWW (Television Wales & West), were on the right, at Pontcanna. Don't know about you, but I'd completely forgotten Mini pick-ups! *Alan Jarvis*

Left: The June Miners' Gala led to traffic diversions, and Corporation bus 430 is on a diversion via Neville Street in 1975 to get to the bus station. When new in 1965 this Guy Arab V was fitted with a Ruston Paxman air-cooled engine, which (amongst other things) meant it had no heater. By the time this picture was taken it had received a Gardner engine from a withdrawn 1948 Bristol KW6G, which just goes to show the durability of that engine make. *Mike Street*

Above right: Sloper Road bus garage (nowadays the headquarters of Cardiff Bus) sets us off westwards from the city centre. City of Cardiff Transport had a habit of buying unique bus types, and these Alexander-bodied AEC Swifts of 1968 were a case in point, if 20 buses can be called unique. They started driver-only operation — now the standard way to operate buses — in 1970. The first, 506, is seen in December 1971 *John Wiltshire*

Below right: As a result of this buying policy City of Cardiff Transport had a fascinating variety of buses. Again at Sloper Road, this line-up gives an idea of the diversity still evident in 1971. From right to left are 471, a 1966 Alexander-bodied Guy (one of 37 of a type unique to Cardiff), 378, a 1961 East Lancs-bodied AEC Regent V, 574, a nearly-new MCW-bodied Daimler Fleetline and, finally, 490, a 1968 Park Royal-bodied Fleetline. Almost incredibly, of this fine selection from the UK's bus-building industry only two manufacturers — Alexander and East Lancs — survive. *John Wiltshire*

Above: Lurking behind the railway tracks beyond the main westward Cowbridge Road was the Sanatorium Road terminus, taking its name from a tuberculosis sanatorium there. It developed into a light-industrial area, including a dairy where your author spent some happy months on the bottle line. Seen in 1965, bus 61 was one of 10 Daimler CVD6s delivered in 1948 and fitted with old bodies. In 1957 they were all rebodied with these rather nice Longwell Green bodies built in Bristol, which were 8ft wide on 7ft 6in-wide chassis, as you can see. Tellingly, one or two of them ended up on their sides after accidents! They were known as 'Splott Bombers', due to their regular use on the 7/7A services to Splott and the distinctive sound of their Daimler engines. *John Woodward*

Right: Another view of Sanatorium Road terminus, this time in 1973, with bus 573, one of the splendid MCW-bodied Leyland-engined Fleetlines known to crews as 'K liners', owing to their K-suffix registrations. In the background is a part of Landsdowne Hospital, which has since been demolished and replaced by housing. There is also a fine example of a Corporation bus stop. *John Woodward*

Left: Our journey now takes us along the main Cowbridge Road through Canton, then the major thoroughfare westwards. This was host to a very high frequency of buses, with one literally always in sight. Cardiff's last trolleybus, 287 of 1955, passes the end of Egerton Street in December 1967. Despite the limited degree of snow clearance on this main highway, people do not seem particularly bothered and are just getting on with the job. *Alan Jarvis*

Right: Victoria Park terminus was for many years the staging-post for Ely, being the point at which one changed from tram to motor bus. The terminal bay for the 5 and 8 trolleybuses (left) was equipped with a magnificent brick shelter set into the park; the No 10 trolleybuses and less-frequent motor buses arrived from behind the photographer, necessitating a sprint to the bus stop near the trolleybus on the left if one turned up first. In the trolleybuses' heyday this point was served by no fewer than 32 an hour! In this 1965 scene an 8 sets off for Royal Oak as an outbound 10B for Ely, not quite halfway to its destination, waits while the crew of a terminating 5 move the booms of their bus onto the correct wire, having failed to operate the power frog (that's points to you and me). *John Woodward*

Right: Approaching Victoria Park from Ely in the December 1967 snow, BUT/East Lancs trolleybus 286 has just passed the local branch of a Cardiff institution, Clark's Pies. There was heated rivalry between supporters of this branch and that at Grangetown over which was best. Thankfully the firm survives and prospers, having a worldwide following! The bus is about to pass the 'Granville' emporium — vital for the supply of local confectionery needs. Again, life seems to go on without massive snow clearing, and the covering of the bus demonstrates that it has no heaters; indeed, Cardiff's first buses with heaters didn't arrive until 1959. Just visible on the skyline is the water tower at Pentrebane. Oh, by the way … Victoria Park 'Clarksies' are best. *Alan Jarvis*

Having just passed Ely Paper Mills and under the railway branch to Radyr, BUT/East Lancs trolleybus 228 in the December 1967 snow heads off towards Victoria Park with its own covering of snow. The tree on the right would, with a few lights, make a splendid Christmas tree!
Alan Jarvis

Right: Cowbridge Road crosses the main ex-GWR railway line at Ely Bridge, where 286, fated to be Cardiff's last service trolleybus, is seen passing through the much simpler junction of the times in December 1969, mere days before the trolleys finished. Following the bus is a Mk 1 Ford Cortina, while on the left can be seen contemporary fashions and a Victoria Laundry Van.
John Wiltshire

Below right: Running along the overhead wires, the trolley-heads at the end of the trolley-poles that picked up the electricity to power the vehicle tended to generate rather a lot of, well, muck, over the back of the bus. Crossing Ely Bridge in November 1969, BUT 218 demonstrates this clearly!
John Wiltshire

Left: The 10A/B trolleybus routes, serving the Ely estate, represented the only major extension beyond the old tram network. It had been intended to extend trams there, and in the estate's main road, Grand Avenue, ample space was devoted to a central reservation for trams. Mr Forbes put paid to the idea in 1929, citing a cost of £59,000, but electric traction finally arrived in 1955 with the final expansion of the trolleybus system. BUT/East Lancs 279, one of the trolleys bought for this route, makes its way along Grand Avenue in August 1969. *John Wiltshire*

Below: Another view of the Grand Avenue central reservation in 1965, and this time something a little different. Motor bus 342, an East Lancs-bodied Daimler CVG6 typical of Cardiff's purchases in the mid-1950s, makes its way back into the city on the very infrequent service from St George's. *John Woodward*

The 10A/B trolleybus routes described a huge circle around Ely, and if you didn't take the Grand Avenue route you continued along Cowbridge Road. Along here you would pass the huge head office and central works of Western Welsh at 253 Cowbridge Road West, which during the summer months also acted as a coach depot (this being sited in the shed behind the double-decker in this view). Seen in October 1971, one of four very attractive Duple Alpine Continental-bodied Leyland Leopard coaches new in 1963 has been prepared — in the NBC corporate coach style of the time — for transfer to Black & White Motorways of Cheltenham. Behind is one of Western Welsh's agreeable-looking AEC Renowns. All this has now gone, the whole site having been redeveloped, and no trace remains of all the activity that once took place here. *Mike Street*

Right: The farthest extremity of the route on Cowbridge Road and pretty much the farthest extremity of the city was the Green Farm Road junction. About to climb virtually the only serious gradient on the system, 286 turns off Cowbridge Road in August 1969. This junction is a much busier and more complex affair today! *John Wiltshire*

Below right: Also in August 1969, 285 leaves Green Farm Road to return to the city centre, showing how this was very much the edge of town in those days. Note the red 'TROLLEYBUS' sticker in the back window, warning other trolleybus drivers not to overtake! *John Wiltshire*

Galas etc

Annual Miners' Galas brought all sorts of buses until they ceased during the miners' strike of the early 1980s

Rare visitors to Cardiff were buses of Gelligaer Urban District Council. Whilst its heartland was the area around Hengoed, Gelligaer nevertheless participated in the mighty joint route between Newport and Rhymney Bridge, which required double-deckers. In 1971 it caused a stir by buying three of these Northern Counties-bodied

Bristol VRTs — a racy choice for a pretty staid operator. No 41 is seen in a muddy Sophia Gardens for the 1972 Miners' Gala. More usual fare in Cardiff was the Rhondda AEC Regent V standing next to it on a similar mission. *Mike Street*

Also rare in Cardiff were double-deckers of Swansea-based South Wales Transport, which company's 891, an impressive Park Royal-bodied AEC Renown, is seen entering Sophia Gardens for the June 1972 Miners' Gala. *Mike Street*

Left: Buses of United Welsh, based in Neath, were also uncommon in Cardiff, but the Miners' Gala brought these to the city too. By 1973 the company had been absorbed into South Wales Transport and this unusual Bristol FSF — a Lodekka variant favoured by United Welsh — had become South Wales 966. It is seen passing along King Edward VII Avenue, in the heart of the imposing Civic Centre. *Mike Street*

Below: Major rugby matches brought folk from far and wide and gave bus enthusiasts who were able to resist the match a field-day. From faraway Pembroke Dock, Silcox, to this day a major operator in West Wales, has sent this unusual Bristol LH with attractive Plaxton bus bodywork. Although this was bought new, Silcox, which had benefited from the construction of the oil refineries at Milford Haven, was more famous for its variety of second-hand buses and its own rebuilds. The bus is parked up in Cathays Park, another part of the grand Civic Centre. Anyway, why bother with the game? Wales *always* won in those days! *Mike Street*

Now this is an indulgence. Yes, it's the 1973 Miners' Gala and it's in Sophia Gardens, but really it's a ploy to try and explain why buses were interesting in those days. On paper, these buses would seem the same, both being forward-entrance Northern Counties-bodied AEC Regent Vs, bought by companies that were commonly managed and, indeed, had by now merged. But just look at all the detail differences! There were obviously very different ideas as to how destinations should be set out, for example. And clearly, by the arrangement of vents on Western Welsh 707 (left), that company felt it should keep its passengers cool and drivers warm, whereas Rhondda, with its 495 (right), thought the exact opposite! I prefer the Western Welsh version. *Mike Street*

(Very) Out and About

Stretching 'Streets of Cardiff' a bit

Left: Cardiff Corporation's buses wandered far afield, and one of the more delightful expeditions was the route out to Hensol Castle through the charming Vale of Glamorgan, Cardiff's stockbroker belt. At the terminus, a good 10 miles out from the city centre, in 1964 is Alexander-bodied Crossley 51. Giving an idea of the decline in bus use, in the 1960s three of these buses left the bus station at 1pm, one going to St Fagans, one to Peterston or Pendoylan and the third all the way. Nowadays only a few journeys are run each day, using 30-seaters. *John Woodward*

Below: St Fagans actually generated more journeys than Hensol Castle, being closer to the city and home to the Welsh Folk Museum, destination of many a school trip. It's just to the right of this rare view of a Corporation single-decker more usually found making its way to Penarth. No 145 was a Longwell Green-bodied Leyland Tiger Cub new in 1957 and seen on a cold and slushy day in 1965. *John Woodward*

Above: Daimler 342 out in the sticks to the west of Cardiff, passing The Drope, in 1965. It has just crossed over the Barry–Wenvoe–Creigiau–Pontypridd railway line, since replaced by the link road from Culverhouse Cross to Junction 33 on the M4. The Drope itself is now the terminus of a high-frequency city service. *John Woodward*

Right: Out in the sticks to the east, Cardiff buses ventured occasionally to Marshfield, Guy Arab IV/East Lancs 323 here being dressed up for such a trip. Along with similarly bodied Daimler 342 in the previous picture this gives an idea of Cardiff's mid-'50s standard bus, a fleet of 54 being built up. Have to confess, it's actually on an enthusiast trip in Llantwit Major in May 1973, but that place is served by Cardiff's buses now, so that's my excuse. *Mike Street*

Perhaps the most spectacular of the out-of-town routes was the 36 from Cardiff to Tredegar, which was operated jointly by Cardiff, Caerphilly and West Mon councils and even had its own tickets. A low bridge necessitated the use of low-height buses with uncomfortable four-abreast seating upstairs. Caerphilly's 34. a Massey-bodied Leyland PD3, is seen in 1971 in Wood Street, about to enter the bus station at the end of its marathon trek. By this time Wood Street had become one-way, the other carriageway being used for parking. *John Wiltshire*

Just leaving Cardiff along Manor Way in May 1971 is West Mon 22, a Willowbrook-bodied Leyland PD2 heading for Tredegar. West Mon was an amalgamation of the Bedwellty and Mynythislwyn urban district councils and had originally adopted a livery of very dark maroon, but from 1968 that gave way to this blue-and-white scheme. The bus is approaching the point where today can be found the busy Junction 32 of the M4. The company survives today as Islwyn Borough Transport. Note the simpler road-works signage of the day. *John Wiltshire*

One of the strange traditions of bus operators is to run a joint service meeting in the middle, then turfing passengers off to change buses to continue through. It's called a 'connecting service'. Cardiff and Caerphilly did this on the top of Caerphilly Mountain at the Traveller's Rest, a hostelry thankfully still very much with us. Here, in 1965, splendid Cardiff Regent V/East Lancs No 381 connects with Caerphilly No 6, an all-Leyland Royal Tiger. A lady shopper transfers for Caerphilly whilst a dog does the same for Cardiff. Note the old 'Road Narrows' sign … and it did! *John Woodward*

Christmas Time is Here Again

Pretty lights and all that

Part of the joy of Christmas was Cardiff's illuminated trolleybuses. With their lights and flags on the booms they created a cheering sight on cold winter evenings. They also made an appearance for shopping festivals. AEC/Northern Counties 201, seen here in 1965 at a traffic-free Victoria Park, shows the light fittings, which on these 7ft 6in-wide buses could be attached to the sides as well; on the later, 8ft-wide buses such fittings could only be on the front. *John Woodward*

Above: Christmas lights in St Mary Street, looking towards the Castle, in January 1968. *Alan Jarvis*

Right: Christmas lights in Queen Street, looking east, in December 1967. *Alan Jarvis*

Above: And what an illuminated trolleybus looked like, although this is Bruce-bodied BUT 262 dressed up as the last one during final trolleybus week in January 1970. It is parked by Graham Buildings, in Newport Road opposite the library, where a display about the trolleybuses was being held. Seems a suitable place to end. *Alan Jarvis*

Back cover: At the Crwys Road/Albany Road/ City Road junction the trolleybuses for Roath Park set off eastwards, whilst those for Gabalfa carried on. Here BUT 274 approaches the junction from Gabalfa with the wrong destination display! Shorn of its chimneys, the pub behind survives today but has lost its Royal title; it is now named 'Scream' (a not unnatural reaction to its new black-and-yellow paintwork), and the products of Hancock's brewery are no longer available. Jothams outfitters, immortalised on the side of 274, was where everyone got his/her school uniform. *Alan Jarvis*